Dear Sister Friend

Dear Sister Friend

A Letter of Love and a Call to Action

Kim Morrow

Dear Sister Friend: A Letter of Love and a Call to Action

Cover Art: Panagiotis Lampridis
Illustrations: Ricky V. Castillo
Interior Layout Design: Jake Muelle
Author Photo: Zoom Studio, Pearland, TX

Published by Lamp Oil Publishing Pearland, TX 77584 Printed in the United States of America

ISBN: 978-1-7336513-0-1

Dedication

To God, I surrender my voice to you.

Contents

Foreword

Not sisters by blood, but sisters by heart
—Author Unknown

I, Stephanie D. Miller, am the mother of two grown daughters. Being the youngest girl birthed by my mother, my formative years were spent in a house lathered in testosterone. My relationships with other females held a different perspective because my sister is seventeen years older than me – old enough to be my mother but too old to be a "sister." With God's grace I was able to develop healthy relationships with women I choose to call my **Sister Friends**.

Never before has the time been right for a book like ***Dear Sister Friend: A Letter of Love and a Call to Action*** than now. Kim Morrow shares the Heart of God for those who are His daughters.

Why? Kim's message to women is so clear.

Women are created to be nurturers, creators, supporters and so much more. However, we face certain **problems**:

- Division
- Diversion
- Disagreement

In my role as either counselor, psychotherapist or mentor I have found there are no wounds so deep as those inflicted from those women who turned from friend to foe. Let me be honest, sometimes the wrong inflicted is perceived rather than real. Nonetheless, the effect is the same. Sadly, the pain is passed on from generation to generation. The pain is often encapsulated in mistrust of those who can help the most. Dear Sister Friend is a much-needed tool for emotional and spiritual healing. It presents some viable **solutions**:

- Discernment
- Wise Decisions
- Prayer

Contrast these with the prevalent culture of today evident in the various reality show franchises and other influences. Unfortunately, the absence of mothering and mentoring has led to new norms that carry anxiety, depression, anger and pain.

The stories presented in Dear Sister Friend along with Scriptures, prayer and questions for personal reflection are the foundation for lasting transformation and wholeness in Abba Father.

> So here's what I want you to do, God helping you: Take your everyday, ordinary life—your sleeping, eating, going-to-work, and walking-around life—and place it before God as an offering. Embracing what God does for you is the best thing you can do for him. Don't become so well-adjusted to your culture that you fit into it without even thinking. Instead, fix your attention on God. You'll be changed from the inside out. Readily recognize what he wants from you, and quickly respond to it. Unlike the culture around you, always dragging you down to its level of immaturity, God brings the best out of you, develops well-formed maturity in you.
>
> Romans 12:1-2 The Message

Are you ready to take a look in the window of your soul and mirror of your heart and do the work? I am. Join me and invite your sisters.

Stephanie D. Miller, MA
Mother, Sister Friend & Daughter of the King

Preface

When I first thought about writing a book the topic was about women and friendship. How to be a better friend, how we hurt each other intentionally and often times unintentionally.

My premise was based on things that had been done to me and on what I had knowingly done to others. I had no intentions to name individuals who had wronged me or vice versa but just to demonstrate a "better", more "friendly" way of handling the circumstance or issue.

I mentioned writing the book to a group of friends and they were encouraging. I had a premise and I even had a title for the book but somehow, I never got around to writing it. As a matter of fact, I was in a complimentary coaching session and this was one of the things I listed that I would accomplish. That was in 2009 or 2010.

Many years would go by but I always kept the thought that I must write this book, I must write this book...

In 2016, I finally put pen to paper while sitting under the hair dryer at the beauty salon.

As I started to write God poured out His message! At first glance it looked like I had wasted all those years that I could have written the book but it turns out that they were not wasted at all! One of my favorite scriptures is Jeremiah 29:11 (NIV)- For I know the plans I have for you declares the Lord, plans to prosper you and not to harm you, plans to give you a hope and a future.

During those years that I was not writing "my" book, God was working His plan in me. He was grooming me, pruning me, burning away the impurities of old thought patterns and hurts that needed to go in order for me to move into the place He had for me. In order for me to execute His plan I needed to submit "my" plans, "my" book to His will so that His better, more perfect plan could be a blessing to me and all His daughters.

Acknowledgments

To God, I give all thanks for my being and as I get closer to Him my life's purpose is revealed and I am so overjoyed in His presence.

To Jesus, the Messiah, I give all thanks and glory for my salvation and for preparing a place for me in His kingdom. I excitedly look forward to His return.

To the Holy Spirit, I give all thanks. I cannot fully express the joy I have in Him as my comforter and adviser. His presence is with me and I am so blessed.

To my Mom, Brenda, there is not another person on this earth that loves me as you do. Your love and support are endless. In addition to all the things you've taught me, including compassion for others, you also passed on your love of reading and writing and I am forever grateful.

To my Dad, Charles, Sr., I am blessed to have the analytical skills and healthy sense of humor you passed on to me. Being able to think on one's feet and have a sense of humor is like a mental swiss army knife… it can help you get through a lot of stuff.

To my grandmother, Mildred, I love you much. Thank you for your love and support.

To my siblings, Charles, Jr., Patty, Isaac and LaQuita. Thank you always for your love and support. You all bring joy, humor and love to my life.

In memory of Tanya and Heath, my sister and brother who are already in Heaven, I know we will be together again.

To my nieces, Jasmine, Jadelyn and Jerrin you have brought indescribable love and joy to my life. Your mom gave Mom and I three precious gifts. I love you with all my heart.

To all my extended family that have sown into my life and continue to pray for me as I take this faith walk, I love and thank you. I would like to extend a special thanks to my cousin Judy, my Aunt Myrna and her son Eugene for being used of God to open up doors on my behalf.

To Anita, my friend and sister. As the oldest child in my family, I didn't have an older sister but when we met in 1988 all of that changed. We became family and I cannot thank you enough for all the love, kindness and support you have given to me and my family.

I am so blessed to have been given the gift of true friendship for over 30+ and 20+ years respectively—(Pam, Janice, Vickie, Andrea, ReKina, DeLisa, Sophia, Agatha, Jessica, Paula, Linda, Hue, Kathryn, Myco and Louis)

To two angels that were introduced to me as I started this journey, Ashley and Stephanie. Thank you does not fully express how grateful I am for all of your input, support and prayers. You extended yourselves to help me and I am forever grateful for your generosity of spirit.

To Linda, my stylist and sister on this kingdom journey, thank you. You are an inspiration as a woman of God and entrepreneur. I love our talks. God has mighty plans for your life. We are on this faith walk together.

To my Pastor and First Lady Dr. Charles E. Perry, Jr. and Charlette Perry—Word of Restoration International Church, Rosharon, TX, thank you for bringing the uncompromised Word of God spoken in love. I am blessed to sit under your teaching.

Introduction

Dear Lord,

Let your Word shine through, use me as a vessel to deliver your message of forgiveness, healing and restoration to your daughters.

Jesus when you taught us to pray you taught us to ask our Heavenly Father to forgive our trespasses as we forgive those who trespass against us. Help us to understand the principle of this verse. That our Heavenly Father will forgive us with the same measure that we forgive those around us. And dear Lord as we seek your face give us a heart of obedience. A heart willing to say – yes Lord, not my will but, your will be done. As we walk in your will we find freedom, we find forgiveness, we find wholeness.

We thank you Father. By faith, let your will be done on earth as it is in heaven. United in faith and obedience there is nothing your people, your daughters can not do. Amen.

———•——

Dear Sister Friend,

I believe we are going into a time of revival where God's people will rise up and glorify His Name in all the earth. It's time to prepare.

As our Savior's return nears, we must take up our swords and fight all manner of wickedness. If a house is divided against itself, that house cannot stand. Mark 3:25 (NIV). Dear sisters it is more important than ever to stay vigilant.

A key tactic used by our spiritual foe, Satan, is division. Division is used to divide and conquer. How much focused energy can we put into fighting him and his army when we are so "busy" fighting among ourselves? What exactly are we fighting about?

Diversion is also a key tactic of the enemy. If he can get us to switch our focus from the true battle to some other meaningless effort, then he gains an advantage. Believe me, while we are focused on foolishness his focus has not changed – to wound, kill and destroy the elect of God.

Let's take a look at some ways that Satan uses division and diversion to distract God's daughters from the mission. But more importantly, we will explore how to get back our focus on the mission!

Charge!

How many times have you heard a woman say, "I don't fool around with women", "I only have male friends" or to say it plainly, "I don't have female friends"?

As women we can provide a laundry list of reasons as to why we do not have or do not want any female friends –

- They Are Too Messy
- You Can't Trust Them
- They Think They're Better Than Me
- They Are So Mean

Let's explore the four categories above to see what lies underneath. On the path of healing we will apply First Aid to our wounds. Wounds that have been unattended to for far too long, wounds that everyone around us can see and smell.

The Great Physician can heal all our wounds. It's time for a house call!

Gossip

CHAPTER 1

They Are Too Messy

———◦◦●◦◦———

We have said or heard another woman say she does not have female friends because "they" are too messy. It is such a common statement that most folks don't even question what the speaker means by "messy". Furthermore, how many of us stop to ask who the "they' is in the scenario? I don't mean idle gossip. I am referring to actually exploring or probing deeper. How did the conflict start? Think back, is it possible that the "they" is you? Is it possible that you have inflicted as much pain on yourself as others have inflicted on you?

The Bible tells us that our words actually do matter. But I tell you, on the day of judgment people will have to give an accounting for every careless or useless word they speak. Matthew 12:36 (AMP).

STORY 1

Heavy Load

Rochelle and Trina live in the same neighborhood where their children attend school together. As a result, the ladies became fast friends.

Usually three times a week, after dinner, when their families have settled down, they go for a walk. It's a time where they can get in some exercise and have a little girl chat.

One evening Rochelle noticed that Trina was not very talkative. If she brought up a topic either Trina did not respond or gave a one-word response. This went on for awhile and it didn't take Rochelle long to figure out something was wrong. But what?

Eventually they came to a park bench and Rochelle motioned for them to take a break. As they sat Trina just looked out into the distance. It seemed like she did not want to meet Rochelle's eyes.

Despite Trina's resistance, Rochelle pressed to know what was bothering her. She assured her whatever it was that it would be okay and that she could tell her anything. When Trina finally relented, with tears in her eyes she told Rochelle what was bothering her.

While Trina was out earlier in the day, running errands, she saw her husband leaving out of a restaurant with a colleague. It was not unusual for him to have business lunches so she checked herself in the mirror and got out of the car to speak to them. She was stunned at what she saw next...

Instead of shaking his colleague's hand he leaned in, embraced him and gave him a tender kiss on the lips. The tender lingering kiss of a lover.

In that instance the family, the life, the world that Trina thought she had was over.

Trina was in shock, trying to process what she had just witnessed. As she pulled into her driveway, she had the strange feeling of not knowing how she had gotten there. She had no recollection of the drive and must have simply been going on autopilot.

Trina had gone through her daily routine of picking up the kids, helping them with homework and preparing dinner. When her husband got home, he greeted her and the kids as he did every day. In the kitchen, he grabbed her from behind and nuzzled her neck as he told her that he loved her. With every word, every gesture, she felt as if she was being stabbed.

As Trina finished her tale Rochelle was speechless. When they arrived back home, Rochelle embraced Trina and told her to call her if she needed anything at all. She also said that she would be praying for Trina and her family.

Throughout the next week, Trina was still running on autopilot. Although she was visibly distant, she had not yet told her husband what she had witnessed.

One afternoon when she picked the kids up from school her son seemed to be very upset as he got into the car. Trina asked him what was wrong and of course he said, "nothing". Later she went up to his room to check on him. He was laying on his bed looking up at the ceiling. She asked her son to please tell her what was bothering him.

He eventually told her what the kids were saying at school about his dad. He had also gotten into a scuffle with Rochelle's son, who had started the rumor that the other kids were spreading.

Two-faced

CHAPTER 2

You Can't Trust Them

———◆◆◆———

Having to ask someone for advice places us in a vulnerable position. Perhaps that is why some people don't trust others enough to confide that they don't have or know all the answers. Some of us would rather pretend and take our chances rather than be transparent. Some would rather pretend than open themselves up to possible ridicule and shame should their particular issue "get out."

Seeking advice is like most things, there are two sides to every coin. Seeking advice can be wise, enlightening or freeing. Seeking advice can also be ill advised, dangerous and/or disastrous. It really depends on the source of the information received and also how the individual entrusted with your personal details handles the information.

When Joshua sent out two spies to check out the land, especially Jericho, they had to hide in the harlot's house and trust that she would not betray their position. In truth the spies had to put trust in Rahab and Rahab had to put trust in the spies that her family would not be harmed as a result of helping them. Rahab proved to be trustworthy and she and her family were blessed. Joshua 2:1-24 (NIV); Matthew 1:1-17 (NIV)

Likewise, I can think of an example in the Bible where trust in someone was misplaced. For example, in the story of Sampson and Delilah Judges 16:15-19 (NIV). Samson confided in the Delilah as to the source of his great strength. He paid dearly for his decision when she betrayed him.

What happens when your "trusted" confidant doesn't handle your issue with care?

Story 2

Do You Have a Minute?
I need some advice...

Penelope, Maxine and Anne worked together for 10 years. Over the years they shared many details of their lives with one another including spouses, children and of course the job.

During a typical day, Penelope, Maxine and Anne went for a coffee break to step away from work and decompress for a while. They ordered and took a seat nearby. None of the ladies were exactly happy with the way things were going at the company so that was the topic of conversation for the day.

During their chat Penelope confided in the ladies that she was considering looking for a new job. In fact, she had lined up a couple of phone interviews. Penelope was so excited! Her excitement was contagious and everyone in the little group celebrated the possibility of a new opportunity with her. Things were looking up!

A day or so later Maxine mentioned to Anne that she thought that their manager needed to know that she was about to lose a valuable member of the team. The team could not afford to lose Penelope, as she was highly skilled. Surely their manager would do something to keep that from happening if she only knew Penelope intended to leave.

Anne surprised Maxine by telling her, "No." "The information that Penelope confided should not be told to management or anyone else. When or if Penelope decides to take action, it is her right and responsibility to share that information when she is ready." Their conversation ended but obviously it still weighed heavily in Maxine's thoughts...

Two weeks later Penelope asked Anne if she had shared the confidential conversation with anyone and Anne told her, "No." She had not shared the information.

Shortly thereafter, Penelope got fired.

Them vs Me

CHAPTER 3

They Think They're Better Than Me

————◆━━■━━◆————

I t seems like since time began this issue has been a thorn in the side of many. Remember Cain and Abel? Classical, biblical example of what can happen when we compare ourselves to others Genesis 4:1-16 (NIV). Why do we do it ladies? Does it ever really end well? I'm going to jump out on a limb here and say, "No."

We see similar stories in the Bible, in the movies and in our daily lives. The practice of comparing yourselves to others can lead to the destruction of others but especially oneself.

What about the story of the 12 spies? Numbers 13:1-33 (NIV) Moses sent them out to explore the land of Canaan. The 12 spies felt small and inadequate when comparing themselves to the inhabitants of Canaan. So, when they returned to give their report to Moses, they presented a scenario that seemed insurmountable for the children of Israel. Sometimes that is how we feel about ourselves, that we don't quite measure up.

However, Caleb had a different opinion, a different outlook and vision.

Caleb said, "Let's go now and take possession of the land. We should be more than able to conquer it." Numbers 13:30 (NIV)

When we get stuck in the quicksand of "they think they are better than me" we have to also stop and think do I think "they" are better than me? Is that why I am so annoyed, so hurt, so angry?

Story 3

It's okay to have standards but it's not okay to put down others, yourself either.

Olivette Boudreaux was raised in an influential and wealthy family. As a child she was blessed to be able to go to the best schools. Olivette was a stellar student and she worked very hard to keep her grades up and to make her family proud.

Although the family had means, Olivette was raised to be humble and respectful of others. She was not entitled. She knew how blessed she was and was mindful that not everyone had the same opportunities.

Julianna Smyth and Olivette had been classmates since elementary school. Now they were both on the cusp of graduating from high school and going on to college.

Unlike Olivette, Julianna exploited the fact that her family was wealthy and influential. She was accustomed to getting her way and she made sure that those who wished to remain in her "good" graces knew it.

So, when Olivette was nominated for Homecoming Queen, Julianna went on a campaign to undermine her to ensure that she would prevail in becoming Homecoming Queen instead. After all she was entitled to be homecoming queen as were her two older sisters and her mom before her. Who did Olivette think she was? More than that, Julianna thought, doesn't she know who I am? The nerve!

Julianna began her character attack by appealing to what the image of a homecoming queen should be according to her and then contrasting that image with Olivette.

Julianna used every tool available to her, low-tech and high-tech. First, she hired a private investigator to take pictures of Olivette while she volunteered at the homeless shelter and also while she looked through clothes at a second-hand thrift store.

She launched a social media campaign and she created high-end goody bags to entice the students to vote for her. The bags she passed out didn't just have the typical candy and such. Her bags included gift cards for food and various places the kids liked to hang out at. Some bags even had a little cash.

Julianna even rented an electronic billboard to further entice students to vote for her. She loved passing by and seeing her picture on the "big screen".

Yep, Julianna went all out and did everything in her power to become Homecoming Queen. No matter what Julianna did Olivette kept true to herself and her convictions. That is why the student body liked and admired her so much.

Bullied

CHAPTER 4

They Are So Mean

———◆◆◆———

Bullying is an epidemic. We see it on the news all the time now. Students attacking each other on-line, sometimes anonymous attacks. Unfortunately, in some cases, constant bullying has resulted in individuals taking their own lives in an attempt to escape their torment.

The sad thing is that some of us never outgrew this childish behavior. Do you realize there are adults that are getting bullied at work, in their social circles and even at church every day? Wow! When will this end? Glad you asked.

Luke 6:27-28 (NIV) says - 27 "But to you who are listening I say: Love your enemies, do good to those who hate you, 28 bless those who curse you, pray for those who mistreat you.

STORY 4

Bullying

Nancy was appointed as president of the Women's Guild at church. Nancy has been a loyal member of Greater Authority Non-Denominational Church for approximately 15 years. She is a very active member of the church and serves in a least 3 organizations. Nancy is often called upon to volunteer at various functions and fund raisers.

Renata is also a loyal member of G.A.N.D.C. Renata has been a member of the congregation for 22 years. Like Nancy she is very active in church. She has also served as president of the Women's Guild on 5 separate occasions. The term of the appointment is 2 years and then members nominate and vote for the next president.

Well, it was time for the Annual G.A.N.D.C. Women's Guild Luncheon. Nancy spent the whole weekend preparing the agenda, slides and theme for the Women's Guild Luncheon to present to the members for their input, prior to presenting it to the First Lady of the church for approval.

As Nancy greeted the members and called the meeting to order she laid out the agenda for the day. She was really excited and looking forward to presenting her ideas to the group.

However, as she was about to lay out her ideas for the theme, Renata interjected and announced to the group that she had gone to the First Lady and presented her ideas for the Women's Guild Luncheon and that they had already been approved.

Although disappointed and unhappy about Renata's stunt, Nancy remained composed and orderly. She did not address or challenge the theme or Renata as she felt powerless because the decision had already been made.

Self-image

CHAPTER 5

I am so...

———•◼◖◗◼•———

We have talked about the hurts others have inflicted on us or we have inflicted on others but what about the hurts we inflict on ourselves?

How many times have you spoken negatively about yourself? Such as:

- I'm so fat.
- I'm so skinny.
- I'm too dark.
- I'm not dark enough.

- My hair is too thin.
- My hair it too short.
- My butt is too big.
- Nobody likes me!

Death and life are in the power of the tongue: and they that love it shall eat the fruit thereof. Proverbs 18:21 (KJV).

We have to take hold and be mindful of the things we say not only about others but ourselves as well. Negative speech (self-talk) can paralyze you and keep you from moving forward. Well that won't do, we have work to do and can ill afford to be distracted from our assignments because of self-doubt.

Instead of speaking negatively (death) about yourself practice speaking the Word of God over yourself (life)!

Here are some scriptures to speak over yourself every day. You can place them on the mirror, on the refrigerator, in the car, etc. as a method of meditating on them day and night.

> *I can do all things through Christ who strengthens me.*
>
> Philippians 4:13 (NKJV)

I praise you because I am fearfully and wonderfully made; your works are wonderful, I know that full well.

Psalm 139:14 (NIV)

What, then, shall we say in response to these things? If God is for us, who can be against us?

Romans 8:31 (NIV)

Who will bring any charge against those whom God has chosen? It is God who justifies.

Romans 8:33 (NIV)

Yet in all these things we are more than conquerors through Him who loved us.

Romans 8:37 (NKJV)

The Lord is my light and my salvation; Whom shall I fear? The Lord is the strength of my life of whom shall I be afraid?

Psalm 27:1 (NKJV)

Let no corrupt communication proceed out of your mouth, but that which is good to the use of edifying, that it may minister grace unto the hearers.

Ephesians 4:29 (KJV)

There are so many uplifting scriptures in the Bible. Additional scripture references can be found in Appendix 2.

Summary

I am sure you noticed that in each example Story that no definitive resolution or ending was provided, because in each scenario there could be various outcomes. In addition, by keeping it open-ended it is an invitation for us to delve into a deeper dialog about these or similar stories to better understand each other and be able to move forward in healing.

I want to be clear that I am not advocating that any of us stand around and accept mistreatment from anyone. There are times when it is best to part ways with someone for your safety, for your peace of mind, for your faith journey, etc. But it is important that we guard against the distractions that sometimes disagreement brings. We have been instructed according to Ephesians 4:25-27-32 (NIV) as to how we are to interact with one another:

Therefore each of you must put off falsehood and speak truthfully to your neighbor, for we are all members of one body.

"In your anger do not sin": Do not let the sun go down while you are still angry, and do not give the devil a foothold.

Anyone who has been stealing must steal no longer, but must work, doing something useful with their hands, that they may have something to share with those in need.

Do not let any unwholesome talk come out of your mouths, but only what is helpful for building others up according to their needs, that it may benefit those who listen.

And do not grieve the Holy Spirit of God, with whom you were sealed for the day of redemption.

Get rid of all bitterness, rage and anger, brawling and slander, along with every form of malice. Be kind and compassionate to one another, forgiving each other, just as in Christ God forgave you.

The important thing is that, we all decide everyday how we are going to react to the events that happen in our lives. We make conscious decisions about our actions and responses.

I am encouraging us as the daughters of God to rise above, refuse to be distracted and lured off course by the subtle devices of the enemy.

Division and diversion are key tactics used to divert our attention and to throw us off course. If our enemy, Satan, creates a diversion which results in shifting our focus from the true war then he has successfully put us at a disadvantage. As individuals we each have to make a decision. The war is for your spirit, your salvation and the salvation of your family.

Make no mistake about it, not only do your decisions and your actions have consequences in this world they have eternal consequences as well. Your decisions not only affect your life but have an impact and influence on others as well.

Your eternal life will be spent in one of two places, Heaven or Hell.

According to John 10:10 (NIV):

> *The thief comes only to steal, kill and destroy; I have come that they may have life and have it to the full.*

Satan is fighting for the ultimate prize – **You!**

My dear sister friends it is time to gird up and prepare for war. So, put on the whole armor of God, according to Ephesians 6:10–18 (NIV):

> *Finally, be strong in the Lord and in his mighty power.*
>
> *Put on the full armor of God, so that you can take your stand against the devil's schemes.*
>
> *For our struggle is not against flesh and blood, but against the rulers, against the authorities, against the powers of this dark world and against the spiritual forces of evil in the heavenly realms.*
>
> *Therefore put on the full armor of God, so that when the day of evil comes, you may be able to stand your ground, and after you have done everything, to stand.*
>
> *Stand firm then, with the belt of truth buckled around your waist, with the breastplate of righteousness in place, and with your feet fitted with the readiness that comes from the gospel of peace.*

In addition to all this, take up the shield of faith, with which you can extinguish all the flaming arrows of the evil one.

Take the helmet of salvation and the sword of the Spirit, which is the word of God.

And pray in the Spirit on all occasions with all kinds of prayers and requests. With this in mind, be alert and always keep on praying for all the Lord's people.

Let's go ladies! Have discernment about who your true enemy is and let's march forward into battle.

Stand up daughters of God! Victory is ours!

Victory!

God Bless you my sisters in Christ Jesus, the Messiah,

Kim

APPENDICES

APPENDIX 1

Prayer of Forgiveness

Lord Jesus,

Help me, I don't even know where to start or how to begin to forgive _____
_____
_____.

In my own strength I am not sure I can forgive them but in your strength all things are possible to those that believe.

So now Lord I surrender my hurt, my anger, my shame to you because it is only through surrender that I can be free from this burden.

Father, you know me better than I know myself and sometimes I go back to old hurts and pick them up again. So much so that often times it feels like it just happened, and my anger is rekindled.

Father, once you have forgiven me it is done. You never take your forgiveness back from me. Help me Lord. Help me to know that all I need to do is lay it back at your feet.

You never tire of helping me because you love me. Thank you, Jesus.

When I remember how I wronged _____

_____

_____

_____my

shame is a weight that keeps me bound to my transgression.

Now Father, thank you for empowering me to forgive _____

_____

for _____

and _____

_____.

Likewise, thank you for empowering me to forgive myself for _____

_____

_____

and how I hurt _____.

Thank you for the power and freedom in forgiveness.

In Jesus Name I pray. Amen.

Small Group Study Group Questions

INTRODUCTION -

1. What are some things that can be distractions in our life?

2. Let's explore what the Bible says about distractions. Luke 10:38-42 NKJV

   > *38 Now it happened as they went that He entered a certain village; and a certain woman named Martha welcomed Him into her house.*

[39] *And she had a sister called Mary, who also sat at Jesus' feet and heard His word.* *[40]* *But Martha was distracted with much serving, and she approached Him and said, "Lord, do You not care that my sister has left me to serve alone? Therefore tell her to help me."*

[41] *And Jesus answered and said to her, "Martha, Martha, you are worried and troubled about many things.* *[42]* *But one thing is needed, and Mary has chosen that good part, which will not be taken away from her."*

3. How do we shift our focus to have a more eternal focus vs. natural focus?

CHAPTER 1 –

1. Do you have female friends? If so, do you have many or few?

2. Do you have life-long female friends or short-term acquaintances?

3. What experiences do you think influenced your friendship choices or preferences?

4. Do you often get into disagreements with your friends? If so, what do you think was the

cause of the disagreement(s)? If you don't why do you think you get along so well.

5. Do you get into disagreements with females in general? If so, what do you think was the cause of the disagreement(s)? If you don't what do you think attributes to your successful interaction with others?

6. When you have disagreements, whether frequently or infrequently how do you handle the situation?

7. Let's explore what the Bible says about friends/friendship. Proverbs 18:1 NIV

    An unfriendly person pursues selfish ends and against all sound judgment starts quarrels.

JUDGES 11:26-40 NIV

[26] For three hundred years Israel occupied Heshbon, Aroer, the surrounding settlements and all the towns along the Arnon. Why didn't you retake them during that time? [27] I have not wronged you, but you are doing me wrong by waging war against me. Let the LORD, the Judge, decide the dispute this day between the Israelites and the Ammonites."

²⁸ *The king of Ammon, however, paid no attention to the message Jephthah sent him.*

²⁹ *Then the Spirit of the* LORD *came on Jephthah. He crossed Gilead and Manasseh, passed through Mizpah of Gilead, and from there he advanced against the Ammonites.* ³⁰ *And Jephthah made a vow to the* LORD: *"If you give the Ammonites into my hands,* ³¹ *whatever comes out of the door of my house to meet me when I return in triumph from the Ammonites will be the* LORD'S, *and I will sacrifice it as a burnt offering."*

³² *Then Jephthah went over to fight the Ammonites, and the* LORD *gave them into his hands.* ³³ *He devastated twenty towns from Aroer to the vicinity of Minnith, as far as Abel Keramim. Thus Israel subdued Ammon.*

³⁴ *When Jephthah returned to his home in Mizpah, who should come out to meet him but his daughter, dancing to the sound of timbrels! She was an only child. Except for her he had neither son nor daughter.* ³⁵ *When he saw her, he tore his clothes and cried, "Oh no, my daughter! You have brought me down and I am devastated. I have made a vow to the* LORD *that I cannot break."*

³⁶ *"My father," she replied, "you have given your word to the* LORD. *Do to me just as you promised, now that the* LORD *has avenged you of your enemies, the Ammonites.* ³⁷ *But*

grant me this one request," she said. "Give me two months to roam the hills and weep with my friends, because I will never marry."

[38] "You may go," he said. And he let her go for two months. She and her friends went into the hills and wept because she would never marry. [39] After the two months, she returned to her father, and he did to her as he had vowed. And she was a virgin.

From this comes the Israelite tradition [40] that each year the young women of Israel go out for four days to commemorate the daughter of Jephthah the Gileadite.

PROVERBS 17:17 NIV

A friend loves at all times, and a brother is born for a time of adversity.

PROVERBS 12:26 NIV

The righteous choose their friends carefully, but the way of the wicked leads them astray.

PROVERBS 16:28 NIV

A perverse person stirs up conflict, and a gossip separates close friends.

PROVERBS 17:9 NIV

Whoever would foster love covers over an offense, but whoever repeats the matter separates close friends.

PROVERBS 18:24 NIV

One who has unreliable friends soon comes to ruin, but there is a friend who sticks closer than a brother.

PROVERBS 19:7 NIV

The poor are shunned by all their relatives— how much more do their friends avoid them! Though the poor pursue them with pleading, they are nowhere to be found.

PROVERBS 22:11 NIV

One who loves a pure heart and who speaks with grace will have the king for a friend.

PROVERBS 22:24 NIV

Do not make friends with a hot-tempered person, do not associate with one easily angered,

Proverbs 27:6 NIV

Wounds from a friend can be trusted, but an enemy multiplies kisses.

Proverbs 27:9 NIV

Perfume and incense bring joy to the heart and the pleasantness of a friend springs from their heartfelt advice.

8. How does the Bible say to handle disagreements? 1 Corinthians 6:1-11 NIV

If any of you has a dispute with another, do you dare to take it before the ungodly for judgment instead of before the Lord's people? [2] Or do you not know that the Lord's people will judge the world? And if you are to judge the world, are you not competent to judge trivial cases? [3] Do you not know that we will judge angels? How much more the things of this life! [4] Therefore, if you have disputes about such matters, do you ask for a ruling from those whose way of life is scorned in the church? [5] I say this to shame you. Is it possible that there is nobody among you wise enough to judge a dispute between believers? [6] But instead, one brother takes another to court— and this in front of unbelievers!

7 The very fact that you have lawsuits among you means you have been completely defeated already. Why not rather be wronged? Why not rather be cheated? 8 Instead, you yourselves cheat and do wrong, and you do this to your brothers and sisters. 9 Or do you not know that wrongdoers will not inherit the kingdom of God? Do not be deceived: Neither the sexually immoral nor idolaters nor adulterers nor men who have sex with men 10 nor thieves nor the greedy nor drunkards nor slanderers nor swindlers will inherit the kingdom of God. 11 And that is what some of you were. But you were washed, you were sanctified, you were justified in the name of the Lord Jesus Christ and by the Spirit of our God.

PROVERBS 17:14 NIV

Starting a quarrel is like breaching a dam; so drop the matter before a dispute breaks out.

PROVERBS 18:19 NKJV

A brother offended is harder to win than a strong city, And contentions are like the bars of a castle.

MATTHEW 5:21-26 MSG

21-22 *"You're familiar with the command to the ancients, 'Do not murder.' I'm telling you that anyone who is so much as angry with a brother or sister is guilty of murder. Carelessly call a brother 'idiot!' and you just might find yourself hauled into court. Thoughtlessly yell 'stupid!' at a sister and you are on the brink of hellfire. The simple moral fact is that words kill.*

23-24 *"This is how I want you to conduct yourself in these matters. If you enter your place of worship and, about to make an offering, you suddenly remember a grudge a friend has against you, abandon your offering, leave immediately, go to this friend and make things right. Then and only then, come back and work things out with God.*

25-26 *"Or say you're out on the street and an old enemy accosts you. Don't lose a minute. Make the first move; make things right with him. After all, if you leave the first move to him, knowing his track record, you're likely to end up in court, maybe even jail. If that happens, you won't get out without a stiff fine.*

CHAPTER 2 –

1. How likely are you to ask for advice from a female friend or acquaintance?

2. Why are you more or less likely to ask for advice from a female friend?

3. Have you been betrayed by a confidant? If so, how did that make you feel? Have you forgiven the person that betrayed your confidence? If not, what will it take for you to forgive the person who betrayed you?

4. What do you consider betrayal?

5. Let's explore what the Bible says about forgiveness. Matthew 6:9-15 NKJV

> *⁹ In this manner, therefore, pray:*
> *Our Father in heaven,*
> *Hallowed be Your name.*
> *¹⁰ Your kingdom come.*
> *Your will be done*
> *On earth as it is in heaven.*
> *¹¹ Give us this day our daily bread.*
> *¹² And forgive us our debts,*
> *As we forgive our debtors.*
> *¹³ And do not lead us into temptation,*
> *But deliver us from the evil one.*

For Yours is the kingdom and the power and the glory forever. Amen.

[14] *"For if you forgive men their trespasses, your heavenly Father will also forgive you.* [15] *But if you do not forgive men their trespasses, neither will your Father forgive your trespasses.*

PSALM 25:11 NKJV

For Your name's sake, O LORD, Pardon my iniquity, for it is great.

PROVERBS 19:11 NIV

The discretion of a man makes him slow to anger, And his glory is to overlook a transgression.

6. How can we apply what the Bible says about forgiveness to our lives?

CHAPTER 3 –

1. Has a female ever tried to ruin your reputation to gain an advantage over you? If so, what was the circumstance? What was the outcome?

2. Have you ever tried to ruin another female's reputation? If so, what did you hope to accomplish?

3. Can the damage of false statements be repaired? If so, how?

4. Let's explore what the Bible says about bearing false witness? Exodus 20:16 NIV

> *"You shall not give false testimony against your neighbor.*

PROVERBS 12:17 NIV

> *An honest witness tells the truth, but a false witness tells lies.*

PROVERBS 6:16-19 NIV

> *[16] There are six things the LORD hates, seven that are detestable to him:*
>
> *[17] haughty eyes, a lying tongue, hands that shed innocent blood,*
>
> *[18] a heart that devises wicked schemes, feet that are quick to rush into evil,*
>
> *[19] a false witness who pours out lies and a person who stirs up conflict in the community.*

PROVERBS 14:5 NIV

An honest witness does not deceive, but a false witness pours out lies.

PROVERBS 14:25 NIV

A truthful witness saves lives, but a false witness is deceitful.

PROVERBS 19:9 NIV

A false witness will not go unpunished, and whoever pours out lies will perish.

PROVERBS 21:28 NIV

A false witness will perish, but a careful listener will testify successfully.

5. How can we apply what the Bible says about restoration to our specific circumstances?

CHAPTER 4 –

1. Have you ever been bullied?

2. In what ways have you been a bully? As a child? As an adult?

3. Did you ever get an opportunity to apologize or make amends in some way? If given the opportunity what steps would you take to rectify the offense?

4. Let's explore what the Bible says about how we are to treat one another. Proverbs 12 NIV

> *Whoever loves discipline loves knowledge, but whoever hates correction is stupid.* ² *Good people obtain favor from the LORD, but he condemns those who devise wicked schemes.*
>
> ³ *No one can be established through wickedness, but the righteous cannot be uprooted.*
>
> ⁴ *A wife of noble character is her husband's crown, but a disgraceful wife is like decay in his bones.*
>
> ⁵ *The plans of the righteous are just, but the advice of the wicked is deceitful.*
>
> ⁶ *The words of the wicked lie in wait for blood, but the speech of the upright rescues them.*
>
> ⁷ *The wicked are overthrown and are no more, but the house of the righteous stands firm.*
>
> ⁸ *A person is praised according to their prudence, and one with a warped mind is despised.*
>
> ⁹ *Better to be a nobody and yet have a servant than pretend to be somebody and have no food.*

¹⁰ The righteous care for the needs of their animals, but the kindest acts of the wicked are cruel.

¹¹ Those who work their land will have abundant food, but those who chase fantasies have no sense.

¹² The wicked desire the stronghold of evildoers, but the root of the righteous endures.

¹³ Evildoers are trapped by their sinful talk, and so the innocent escape trouble.

¹⁴ From the fruit of their lips people are filled with good things, and the work of their hands brings them reward.

¹⁵ The way of fools seems right to them, but the wise listen to advice.

¹⁶ Fools show their annoyance at once, but the prudent overlook an insult.

¹⁷ An honest witness tells the truth, but a false witness tells lies.

¹⁸ The words of the reckless pierce like swords, but the tongue of the wise brings healing.

¹⁹ Truthful lips endure forever, but a lying tongue lasts only a moment.

²⁰ Deceit is in the hearts of those who plot evil, but those who promote peace have joy.

²¹ No harm overtakes the righteous, but the wicked have their fill of trouble.

²² The LORD detests lying lips, but he delights in people who are trustworthy.

²³ *The prudent keep their knowledge to themselves, but a fool's heart blurts out folly.*

²⁴ *Diligent hands will rule, but laziness ends in forced labor.*

²⁵ *Anxiety weighs down the heart, but a kind word cheers it up.*

²⁶ *The righteous choose their friends carefully, but the way of the wicked leads them astray.*

²⁷ *The lazy do not roast any game, but the diligent feed on the riches of the hunt.*

²⁸ *In the way of righteousness there is life; along that path is immortality.*

MATTHEW 6:5-14 NKJV

⁵ *"And when you pray, you shall not be like the hypocrites. For they love to pray standing in the synagogues and on the corners of the streets, that they may be seen by men. Assuredly, I say to you, they have their reward.*
⁶ *But you, when you pray, go into your room, and when you have shut your door, pray to your Father who is in the secret place; and your Father who sees in secret will reward you openly.* ⁷ *And when you pray, do not use vain repetitions as the heathen do. For they think that they will be heard for their many words.*

⁸ *"Therefore do not be like them. For your Father knows the things you have need*

of before you ask Him. ⁹ *In this manner, therefore, pray:*

Our Father in heaven, Hallowed be Your name. ¹⁰ *Your kingdom come. Your will be done*

On earth as it is in heaven. ¹¹ *Give us this day our daily bread.* ¹² *And forgive us our debts, As we forgive our debtors.* ¹³ *And do not lead us into temptation, But deliver us from the evil one. For Yours is the kingdom and the power and the glory forever. Amen.*

¹⁴ *"For if you forgive men their trespasses, your heavenly Father will also forgive you.*

1 JOHN 4:7-11 NKJV

⁷ *Beloved, let us love one another, for love is of God; and everyone who loves is born of God and knows God.* ⁸ *He who does not love does not know God, for God is love.* ⁹ *In this the love of God was manifested toward us, that God has sent His only begotten Son into the world, that we might live through Him.* ¹⁰ *In this is love, not that we loved God, but that He loved us and sent His Son to be the propitiation for our sins.* ¹¹ *Beloved, if God so loved us, we also ought to love one another.*

1 JOHN 4:20-21 NKJV

20 If someone says, "I love God," and hates his brother, he is a liar; for he who does not love his brother whom he has seen, how can he love God whom he has not seen? 21 And this commandment we have from Him: that he who loves God must love his brother also.

ROMANS 12:17-21 NIV

17 Do not repay anyone evil for evil. Be careful to do what is right in the eyes of everyone. 18 If it is possible, as far as it depends on you, live at peace with everyone. 19 Do not take revenge, my dear friends, but leave room for God's wrath, for it is written: "It is mine to avenge; I will repay," says the Lord. 20 On the contrary:

"If your enemy is hungry, feed him; if he is thirsty, give him something to drink. In doing this, you will heap burning coals on his head."

21 Do not be overcome by evil, but overcome evil with good.

5. What protection do we have according to the Bible?

CHAPTER 5 –

1. What do think about yourself when you look in the mirror?

2. Do you think your viewpoint matters?

3. Do you feel that way because of something someone else said about you?

4. What is your typical reaction when you are complimented? Are you more apt to say, "Thank You" or are you more apt to downplay it? Why?

5. Let's explore what the Bible says about us?

GENESIS 1:27 NKJV

> So God created man in His own image; in the image of God He created him; male and female He created them.

PSALM 139:13-16 NIV

> [13] For you created my inmost being; you knit me together in my mother's womb. [14] I praise you because I am fearfully and wonderfully made; your works are wonderful, I know that full well. [15] My frame was not hidden from you

when I was made in the secret place, when I was woven together in the depths of the earth. ¹⁶ *Your eyes saw my unformed body; all the days ordained for me were written in your book before one of them came to be.*

PHILIPPIANS 4:13 NKJV

I can do all things through Christ who strengthens me.

PSALM 37:23-24 NIV

²³ *The LORD makes firm the steps of the one who delights in him;* ²⁴ *though he may stumble, he will not fall, for the LORD upholds him with his hand.*

PSALM 23 NKJV

The LORD is my shepherd; I shall not want. ² *He makes me to lie down in green pastures; He leads me beside the still waters.* ³ *He restores my soul; He leads me in the paths of righteousness*

For His name's sake. ⁴ *Yea, though I walk through the valley of the shadow of death, I will fear no evil; For You are* with *me; Your rod and Your staff, they comfort me.* ⁵ *You* prepare a table before me in the presence of my enemies; You anoint my head with oil; My cup runs over. *6* Surely goodness and mercy shall follow me All the days of my life; And I will dwell in the house of the LORD Forever.

EPHESIANS 2:8-10 NKJV

8 For by grace you have been saved through faith, and that not of yourselves; it is the gift of God,

9 not of works, lest anyone should boast. *10* For we are His workmanship, created in Christ Jesus for good works, which God prepared beforehand that we should walk in them.

JOHN 8:1-12 NIV

1 but Jesus went to the Mount of Olives.

2 At dawn he appeared again in the temple courts, where all the people gathered around him, and he sat down to teach them. *3* The teachers of the law and the Pharisees brought in a woman caught in adultery. They made her stand before the group *4* and said to Jesus, "Teacher, this woman was caught in the act of adultery. *5* In the Law Moses commanded us to stone such women. Now what do you say?" *6* They were using this question as a trap, in order to have a basis for accusing him.

But Jesus bent down and started to write on the ground with his finger.[7] When they kept on questioning him, he straightened up and said to them, "Let any one of you who is without sin be the first to throw a stone at her." [8] Again he stooped down and wrote on the ground.

[9] At this, those who heard began to go away one at a time, the older ones first, until only Jesus was left, with the woman still standing there.[10] Jesus straightened up and asked her, "Woman, where are they? Has no one condemned you?"

[11] "No one, sir," she said.

"Then neither do I condemn you," Jesus declared. "Go now and leave your life of sin."

6. How can we change our mindset and see ourselves as God sees us?

SUMMARY -

1. What is your viewpoint on good and evil?

2. Do you believe good people go to heaven? What about evil people? Discuss your viewpoint.

3. Do you believe the Word of God is true? If so, why? If not, why?

4. Let's explore what the Bible says about eternal life. John 3:16–17 NIV

> *¹⁶ For God so loved the world that he gave his one and only Son, that whoever believes in him shall not perish but have eternal life. ¹⁷ For God did not send his Son into the world to condemn the world, but to save the world through him.*

JOHN 17 NIV

> *After Jesus said this, he looked toward heaven and prayed:*
>
> *"Father, the hour has come. Glorify your Son, that your Son may glorify you. ² For you granted him authority over all people that he might give eternal life to all those you have given him. ³ Now this is eternal life: that they know you, the only true God, and Jesus Christ, whom you have sent. ⁴ I have brought you glory on earth by finishing the work you gave me to do. ⁵ And now, Father, glorify me in your presence with the glory I had with you before the world began.*
>
> *⁶ "I have revealed you to those whom you gave me out of the world. They were yours; you gave them to me and they have obeyed your word. ⁷ Now they know that everything you have given me comes from you. ⁸ For I*

gave them the words you gave me and they accepted them. They knew with certainty that I came from you, and they believed that you sent me. *9* I pray for them. I am not praying for the world, but for those you have given me, for they are yours. *10* All I have is yours, and all you have is mine. And glory has come to me through them. *11* I will remain in the world no longer, but they are still in the world, and I am coming to you. Holy Father, protect them by the power of your name, the name you gave me, so that they may be one as we are one. *12* While I was with them, I protected them and kept them safe by that name you gave me. None has been lost except the one doomed to destruction so that Scripture would be fulfilled. *13* "I am coming to you now, but I say these things while I am still in the world, so that they may have the full measure of my joy within them. *14* I have given them your word and the world has hated them, for they are not of the world any more than I am of the world. *15* My prayer is not that you take them out of the world but that you protect them from the evil one. *16* They are not of the world, even as I am not of it. *17* Sanctify them by the truth; your word is truth. *18* As you sent me into the world, I have sent them into the world. *19* For them I sanctify myself, that they too may be truly sanctified.

[20] *"My prayer is not for them alone. I pray also for those who will believe in me through their message,* [21] *that all of them may be one, Father, just as you are in me and I am in you. May they also be in us so that the world may believe that you have sent me.* [22] *I have given them the glory that you gave me, that they may be one as we are one—* [23] *I in them and you in me—so that they may be brought to complete unity. Then the world will know that you sent me and have loved them even as you have loved me.*

[24] *"Father, I want those you have given me to be with me where I am, and to see my glory, the glory you have given me because you loved me before the creation of the world.*

[25] *"Righteous Father, though the world does not know you, I know you, and they know that you have sent me.* [26] *I have made you[e] known to them, and will continue to make you known in order that the love you have for me may be in them and that I myself may be in them."*

1 JOHN 4:1-6 NIV

Dear friends, do not believe every spirit, but test the spirits to see whether they are from God, because many false prophets have gone out into the world. [2] *This is how you can* recognize the Spirit of God: Every spirit that acknowledges that Jesus Christ has come in the flesh is from God, *3* but every spirit that does not acknowledge Jesus is not from God. This is the spirit of the antichrist, which you have heard is coming and even now is already in the world.

4 You, dear children, are from God and have overcome them, because the one who is in you is greater than the one who is in the world. *5* They are from the world and therefore speak from the viewpoint of the world, and the world listens to them. *6* We are from God, and whoever knows God listens to us; but whoever is not from God does not listen to us. This is how we recognize the Spirit of truth and the spirit of falsehood.

JOHN 5:24 NKJV

"Most assuredly, I say to you, he who hears My word and believes in Him who sent Me has everlasting life, and shall not come into judgment, but has passed from death into life.

1 JOHN 5:11-13 NKJV

11 And this is the testimony: that God has given us eternal life, and this life is in His Son. *12* He who has the Son has life; he who *does not have the Son of God does not have life.* [13] *These things I have written to you who believe in the name of the Son of God, that you may know that you have eternal life, and that you may continue to believe in the name of the Son of God.*

GALATIANS 6:7-10 NIV

[7] *Do not be deceived: God cannot be mocked. A man reaps what he sows.* [8] *Whoever sows to please their flesh, from the flesh will reap destruction; whoever sows to please the Spirit, from the Spirit will reap eternal life.* [9] *Let us not become weary in doing good, for at the proper time we will reap a harvest if we do not give up.* [10] *Therefore, as we have opportunity, let us do good to all people, especially to those who belong to the family of believers.*

5. What is our role in this fight between good and evil?

Mighty Warrior of God

APPENDIX 3

Armor of God

———◆◆◆———

14 Stand firm then, with the belt of truth buckled around your waist, with the breastplate of righteousness in place,

15 and with your feet fitted with the readiness that comes from the gospel of peace.

16 In addition to all this, take up the shield of faith, with which you can extinguish all the flaming arrows of the evil one.

17 Take the helmet of salvation and the sword of the Spirit, which is the word of God.

Ephesians 6:14–17 (NIV)

NOTES

NOTES

NOTES

NOTES

NOTES

NOTES

NOTES

NOTES

NOTES

NOTES

References

About The Author

Kim Morrow, a career IT professional, has always loved writing. She has utilized her gift in numerous ways over the years but now she has written her first book – *Dear Sister Friend*.

One of her favorite scriptures is Jeremiah 29:11(NIV) – For I know the plans I have for you declares the Lord, plans to prosper you and not to harm you, plans to give you a hope and a future.

Today as the founder and CEO of Speak Life International LLC she has stepped into her purpose using her voice to help women move into their true destiny.

Kim currently lives in Pearland, a suburb of Houston, TX.

To contact the author for speaking engagements, book readings, to facilitate small group discussions or other special requests you may reach her at: 281-819-4558 or

kim.morrow@speaklifeinternational.com

For more information about the book Dear Sister Friend please go to –

www.dearsisterfriendbook.com

To learn more information regarding upcoming projects please go to –

www.speaklifeinternational.com